WHAT IS YOUR IDEA OF PERFECT HAPPINESS?

What is Your Idea of Perfect Happiness?

CONVERSATIONS INSPIRED BY THE PROUST QUESTIONNAIRE TO INSPIRE YOU

Rossella E. Frigerio

One Blue Dot

Contents

Foreword

Whether we are conscious of it or not, the lives of others inspire how we live our own. To observe how people create, connect, and love, all while remaining open to learning from these different ways of living is to fill yourself up with life-affirming energy. Remain curious, and you will always uncover truths about yourself and our world. Ultimately, you will discover that curiosity is the key to fulfilment.

I have always been fascinated by the diversity of humanity, and have constantly looked for ways to discover what lies behind first impressions. The Proust Questionnaire – a parlour game that was popularised by the French writer Marcel Proust in the late 1800s – offers the perfect opportunity to do just that. Originally a series of 35 questions, the game seeks to uncover the player's true nature. Short questions that are fun, deep, and thought-provoking all at once, their beauty is held in their timelessness – answer them today, answer them again tomorrow, and invariably, your answers will change. The inspiration is constant.

Drawn to this questionnaire, over the years I have used ten of its questions as the basis for my discovery of individuals spearheading a way of life that is rooted in honesty, purity, harmony, and integrity. This book is an edit of conversations that span lives lived everywhere from Beirut to Byron Bay; stories to keep at your fingertips and to leaf through when you are seeking new perspectives at any moment. May they inspire you to live each day fully, lightly, and in constant fascination – now and always.

- Rossella E. Frigerio

1

Aude Giraud

FOUNDER OF ASK A FRENCH, FLORIST, MUSICIAN

Aude Giraud's story is steeped in magic, one that is defined by serendipity and the wonder of storytelling led by intuition. Her floral atelier, Ask A French, tucked away in Singapore's charming Tiong Bahru neighbourhood, is an ode to nature's wild beauty and the romance of classic still life paintings.

Born in France, Aude's heritage is multi-faceted - one that blends the East and West together, and fuses her father's French-Italian roots with her mother's Javanese lineage. Her professional journey has taken many forms - from working as a music and cultural programmer for Radio France, interviewing the likes of Ryan Gosling and Marion Cotillard, to her pursuit of song writing as Flanery (her "second self"), her work has always contained an essence of storytelling. Her clients are both small and personal as well as global and iconic (read Chanel and ERES), and each one shares a love for Aude's unique floral aesthetic that is at once raw and harmonious.

When Aude moved to the island-state of Singapore several years ago, her love for all things botanic took a large turn and blossomed. She founded Ask A French, cultivating and sharing her deep relationship with the natural world through workshops and her personalised bouquets for living spaces and events. Its very opening is testament to her commitment towards living a life guided by intuition. One day, during her first months in Singapore, she was walking along a quiet corner in Tiong Bahru when she noticed a half-open door. Curious, she stepped inside and lay her eyes on what she described as her dream studio. She wondered if the space would ever become available to rent one day, and as she walked away, she felt it would remain just that: a dream. One year later, a property in the neighbourhood was listed on a local online portal and she booked to view it. It was only when she went on site that she realised it was the very same spot that she had set her eyes and heart upon months before. It was a moment that perfectly reflected her personal mantra: always allow your intuition guide you, and try not to be afraid.

What is your idea of perfect happiness?

Flowers, music, nature, and enjoying the little things in life, like a slice of freshly baked lemon cake with a nice cup of coffee or tea. You see, happiness can be easy!

What is your current state of mind?

"On est bien peu de chose et mon amie la rose me l'a dit ce matin."

In other words, we are nothing but a drop of water in the immensity of the ocean.

If you were to die and come back as a person or a thing, who or what would she/he/it be and why?

I would like to come back as Leonard Cohen's guitar. I think it would have a lot to say…

If you could change one thing about yourself, what would it be?

Everything and nothing. Anyway, it's impossible!

What is your greatest regret?

I guess if I looked into it, I might find a few, but, as we say in French, *"Mieux vaut des remords que des regrets."* It means that it's better to try and act than not to act at all.

What is your most treasured possession?

My husband, if you consider that you can own someone, haha!

What is the quality you most like in a man?

Good taste, sense of humour, kindness.

What is the quality you most like in a woman?

That of being a woman and a man at the same time.

What do you consider your greatest achievement?

My music album, 'Oh Boy', that represents the culmination of an intense creative process.

What is your motto?

Things always happen (or not) for a reason. Play and repeat.

2

Anestis Michalis

INTERIOR STYLIST, CREATIVE DIRECTOR

For Athens-based interior stylist and creative director Anestis Michalis, simplicity rooted in nature is the purest expression of creativity. It is an ethos that he has expressed throughout his decades-long career, which began with his creative direction for the pages of *ELLE Decor* and subsequently unfolded into his creative consultancy practice.

The distinct silhouettes of his ceramics are what originally caught our eye and drew us to his work. Singular creations, each is an invitation to experience a deep emotional journey.

"Through each piece, I want to create unique feelings and positive vibes. It can be anything from a deep emotion, but also even a distinct smell that is brought to life in your mind when you see the piece. At the same time, I wish to leave each piece open to each individual's interpretation, asking 'What do you see?' Inevitably, everyone's answer will be different, and that, to me, is where the beauty in each piece lies."

His ceramics capture differing glazes that ooze out of vessels, embodying contrasting elements that point to concepts of 'wrongness', yet which Anestis constantly leaves open to the viewer's interpretation. Each captures the ambiguous space that lies between the finished and unfinished, the earth and the water elements, all while celebrating forms of opposition that these 'creatures' express.

What is your idea of perfect happiness?

We ought to understand that any discussion about happiness and the measurement of happiness has to be grounded in an ethical debate and approach. This is absolutely key for me, since art has a crucial place in society and is inextricably related to human wellbeing.

What is your current state of mind?

It's really hard to identify a state of mind in this precarious moment of radical change.

If you were to die and come back as a person or a thing, who or what would she/he/it be and why?

I believe in the present moment. I was never preoccupied with the idea of the afterlife.

If you could change one thing about yourself, what would it be?

My occasional impulsiveness.

What is your greatest regret?

The only regret I can only articulate is the big box of ice cream I devoured last week!

What is your most treasured possession?

The people that allowed me to become who I am today.

What is the quality you most like in a man?

For me, the human factor cannot be moulded into gender norms.

What is the quality you most like in a woman?

Ditto.

What do you consider your greatest achievement?

Articulating an achievement constitutes a fictitious barrier that prevents me from allowing my practice to evolve and face even greater challenges.

What is your motto?

Don't overthink things. Just get started.

3

Beckielou Brown and Bridget Plant

CO-FOUNDERS OF ALTRA

Years ago, a chance encounter in London led me to Beckielou Brown, and from the moment we connected, her gentle and luminous energy was instantly felt. Pure, genuine and kind, Beckielou is a rare soul. Her bohemian upbringing and distinct way of being, untethered from the predictable and conventional, have forever been a source of inspiration.

When she unveiled her brand of genderless perfumes, Altra, the joy of seeing her work of many years finally revealed to the world was boundless. Co-founded alongside lifelong friend Bridget Plant, Altra is a visionary statement of the future.

Conceived as distinct collections of genderless scents, Altra is an ode to friendship, to transparency, and to a deep-rooted reverence for Nature. While the brand strives to minimise its environmental impact, it honestly and openly accepts that "as an organisation that manufactures consumer products, it's impossible to be truly sustainable." Instead, Altra seeks to be responsible - an approach that in itself speaks volumes about its founders and their commitment to their values.

The brand uncovers a new take on naturals, using pure plant ingredients to evoke an otherworldly feel while remaining committed to its 'no synthetics' vision. In reflection of its futuristic creativity, Beckielou and Bridget have worked with digital artist George Jasper Stone to create immersive environments for each scent. Since launching, Altra has attracted the attention of like-minded retailers across the world, with the likes of Just One Eye in Los Angeles and Universal Providers in London stocking the brand.

In this way, Altra is more than just about perfume. It is the assertion that another - a better way is possible when we make choices that are guided by honesty. Acknowledging that sustainability and consumption are contradictory concepts is the first step in shaping a way of doing business that is not driven by the bottom line alone.

What is your idea of perfect happiness?

Bridget Plant (BP): A still mind, my favourite people, sunshine.

Beckielou Brown (BB): A house full of friends, family, beautiful food, music and laughter.

What is your current state of mind?

(BP): Constant questioning, a whirlwind of activity.

(BB): Truly grateful. This year I got to launch my perfume brand Altra, with my best friend Bridget. Nearly 5 years of dreaming, brainstorming, scent creation, experimentation, creative growth and a LOT of hard work and tough lessons, each one of which I'm extremely grateful for. It feels great to be starting this new chapter with something tangible to share with people. It's not that things are any less hectic, but the joy of seeing how far we've come has energized me for the path ahead.

If you were to die and come back as a person or a thing, who or what would she/he/it be and why?

(BP): Something still and all seeing - an Oak tree perhaps?

(BB): A dog - endless enthusiasm and optimism is the energy I want to come back with!

If you could change one thing about yourself, what would it be?

(BP): To be a calmer version of myself.

(BB): My habit of constantly buying books and only reading the first thirty pages. I have stacks of books all with a page turned in the same place.

What is your greatest regret?

(BP): No regrets

(BB): Not being more present.

What is your most treasured possession?

(BP): The amulets I wear around my neck.

(BB): My freedom.

What is the quality you most like in a man?

(BP): Kindness, strength and the ability to be decisive under pressure.

(BB): Generosity of spirit.

What is the quality you most like in a woman?

(BP): Warmth, razor-like wit and the ability to laugh at oneself.

(BB): The same, for all humans.

What do you consider your greatest achievement?

(BP): My children, my family.

(BB): Attracting amazing people into my life.

What is your motto?

(BP): To go above and beyond (our family's motto).

(BB): Everything is unfolding exactly as it should - trust in the process.

4

Bianca Gregg

CO-FOUNDER OF DEL RAINBOW SHOWROOM

The commercial aspect of the global fashion industry is often perceived as a cutthroat, aggressively competitive arena. A cliquey, insincere space, the aim of selling the next temporary fad dominates over designer camaraderie and sincere respect for clients, the consumer, and our planet. It is a crowded and competitive market, often pushing brands, buyers, retailers and showrooms to brashly churn out and promote fashion labels and products that ultimately create unsustainable and empty desires among the final consumer - all in the name of profit margins and fleeting fashion-coolness.

Quietly, beneath all of this noise and superficiality, leading figures are diligently putting into place the foundations of a new fashion ecosystem, one that is not driven solely by financial gain and trends, but rather, that places the heart and considered intention at the centre of all that revolves around business. Enter the co-founder of Del Rainbow showroom, Bianca Gregg.

Having worked within the fashion industry for over a decade, Bianca became increasingly disenchanted and frustrated with the lack of genuine care and empathy that is held for the human side of the fashion equation. In 2018, alongside her fiancé Arlen Macpherson and armed with a deep conviction that the fashion world could, should, and *must* do better, she launched global sales, consultancy and brand development agency, Del Rainbow, located just a stone's throw away from the beaches of Byron Bay.

At the core of its vision, Del Rainbow champions the exchange of positive energy so that it flows through each step of the fashion cycle. It's not about paying lip service to sustainability. Rather, it looks closely to the people behind the brands and - more importantly - upholds the why they do what they do as expressed through fashion.

Del Rainbow is an extension of Bianca's own vision of life - one that is grounded in honesty, positivity, respect, and an awareness of our place in the world and our interconnectedness with all that surrounds us. Her belief in championing a balance of both the emotional and the intellectual across all aspects of business has brought international retailers to resonate with her distinct philosophy, including Net Sustain by Net-a-Porter, Conscious by Browns, Project Earth by Selfridges, and The Responsible Edit by Matches Fashion.

2020 has proven that the old systems are no longer relevant - including those that once defined the fashion universe. Del Rainbow is a spark of the light that the new world is going to glow of - the uplifting promise of what lies ahead.

What is your idea of perfect happiness?

Following my passion.

What is your current state of mind?

Aligned, balanced and open.

If you were to die and come back as a person or a thing, who or what would she/he/it be and why?

A wild horse. I think horses are the most powerful and majestic beings. They harness femininity and masculinity. The ability to run with a heard and in nature is dreamy.

If you could change one thing about yourself, what would it be?

The amount of hot chips that I eat - this needs to decrease.

What is your most treasured possession?

If dogs count, my two British Bulldogs, Meatloaf and King.

What is the quality you most like in a man?

Awareness of oneself and vulnerability.

What is the quality you most like in a woman?

Grace.

What do you consider your greatest achievement?

Creating Del Rainbow.

What is your motto?

Be Kind, Kinder, Kindest.

5

Clementina Calleri

FOUNDER OF THE PALMIST

Clementina Calleri is the creator of the magical world that is The Palmist. With Italian roots and a life journey that has led her across far-flung corners of the world - from Northern Kenya to Valladolid via

London - she has now settled in Italy for the very first time in her life and opened her creative studio in Milan.

The Palmist is synonymous with eclectic lifestyle wares that embrace everything from fronds-turned-lampshades to antique banners embroidered with vintage silk threads. All are infused with Clementina's desire to bring an uplifting and warm energy into living spaces everywhere.

Her story is a fascinating one. It embraces a love for all that is artisanal and deeply rooted in ancient crafts that speak of a country's unique traditions. With a background in photojournalism, Clementina channels her experiences that count working alongside Coqui Coqui founder, Nicolas Malleville, and supporting children's education in Kenya to create and source one-of-a-kind wares for The Palmist. The result? A rare mix of form, substance, spirituality, and heart.

What is your idea of perfect happiness?

A moment without fear / time spent with artisans in the bush making baskets / having my family reunited / slow travelling.

What is your current state of mind?

Express my creativity in every possible way. Channel the thousands of ideas that come to my mind and transform the best of those into projects and collaborations.

If you were to die and come back as a person or a thing, who or what would she/he/ it be and why?

Hard one. There are so many things and people that I dream of being. If I were to come back as a person, I would love to be a craftswoman in the Japanese mountains - it is such a distant culture from what I have experienced up until now, it would feel like a real discovery to me. If I were to come back as a thing, then I would love to be a giant Magnolia tree.

If you could change one thing about yourself, what would it be?

Definitely my stubbornness. They say that Aries are really hard to convince!

What is your greatest regret?

Taking so much time to understand that my body can't carry the weight of the world.

What is your most treasured possession?

Great question. I have two: a pair of antique Japanese *zōri*, traditional sandals made of straw, which I found in a tiny market in Greece. The second, a Brazilian traditional woven *Xavante Baquités* bag, which I bring everywhere with me.

What is the quality you most like in a man?

Patience.

What is the quality you most like in a woman?

Generosity.

What do you consider your greatest achievement?

Founding The Palmist Club has enabled me to free my creative spirit and to support children's education in Wamba, Northern Kenya, where my family and I built a community school for disadvantaged children aged 2 to 7 in memory of my brother Seba.

What is your motto?

Sorridi sempre - Keep smiling. People will help you; it is the teaching I have always received from my father.

6

Cynthia Louise

CHEF

My path crossed with that of Cynthia Louise quite by chance - as often the most memorable encounters do. A humid weekend afternoon and a late lunch at a café tucked away in the folds of Ubud provided the backdrop to what turned into an unforgettable conversation. It was a mutual friend who brought our tables together that day, and as the hours unfolded, we shared not just lunch but also stories about Bali, food, fashion, and our adventures across the world.

A renowned plant-based chef, it was Cynthia's radiant enthusiasm towards what she does and towards life generally that made the greatest impression. Inspired, over the years, I have observed how this very energy propels her from one success to the next, from writing several best-selling recipe books to partnering with entrepreneur Roger Hamilton to establish a successful restaurant brand. This is what distinguishes Cynthia from the work of others in her field - each sustainable recipe created; each piece of health and life advice given is shared with a generous infusion of genuine love for all that she does, for nature, and for humanity.

From her vast array of courses, classes, retreats and meticulously-researched products, Cynthia seeks to bring us closer to food that is both as pure and as rich in flavour as possible. Her meals are designed to be easy to prepare, no matter where you may live in the world, and are packed with high-vibrational nutrients. Simplicity, acceptance of self and showing up to food just as you are – these are the fundamental elements of Cynthia's philosophy. Her infectious, purpose-filled energy reminds us of the importance that food holds in supporting us through the seasons and changes of life, showing us the immense power that the simple gesture of preparing a meal holds.

What is your idea of perfect happiness?

For me there is no feeling of "perfect" anything. I feel that my state of mind can lift and shift into anything from happiness to sadness. The idea that I can move from worry, lack, loss, and hardship is a great space as it brings out more happiness.

What is your current state of mind?

Joyful.

If you were to die and come back as a person or a thing, who or what would she/he/it be and why?

Me, I would come back as myself. Simply because so far, I have had a magnificent life, and to come back to that after death would be heaven.

If you could change one thing about yourself, what would it be?

I would go to school and start my cooking journey earlier and invest in the art and science of baking.

What is your greatest regret?

Nothing.

What is your most treasured possession?

My heart.

What is the quality you most like in a man?

Kindness, loyalty, truth, strength and willingness.

What is the quality you most like in a woman?

Kindness, loyalty, truth, strength and willingness.

What do you consider your greatest achievement?

Living.

What is your motto?

Today we get to begin again.

7

Daisy Sophia

FOUNDER OF CASTAWAY

Perhaps because it resonates with my tropical childhood, when I came across Castaway - a digital island community steeped in exotic vibes – it immediately felt like home.

Launched by Daisy Sophia, the platform and online shop speak of her journeys across remote corners of the world, from Costa Rica to Sri Lanka through to Indonesia and Australia. Originally from the Netherlands, Daisy inherited her love of travel from her ancestors, who spent years traversing the oceans to explore little-known lands and who lived for years on the island of Curaçao.

Having graduated in Fashion and Branding from the Amsterdam Fashion Institute, Daisy subsequently specialised in curating the branding and visuals for slow-life hospitality and lifestyle brands internationally. It was the springboard into new adventures, weaving a further thread into her travel tapestry.

Castaway reflects Daisy's nomadic spirit and her love for all things handmade, shaped by the hands and lands they come from. Offering a thoughtful selection of lifestyle and skincare products suited to island life – and not only – each has been sourced from skilled artisans everywhere from Hawai'i to Morocco. Polynesian sea urchin necklaces, Mexican prickly pear oil, and Castaway's very own sunglasses all find their space within this palm-leaf-fringed digital space.

Above all, Castaway is about embracing a free-spirited *joie de vivre*, no matter if you live on or off a tropical island. What counts is the warmth of authenticity and a love for all things created to last.

What is your idea of perfect happiness?

To wake up in a hammock on a deserted island surrounded by palm trees. To cut some fresh coconuts by hand. To walk barefoot in the sand while listening to the sound of the ocean every day.

What is your current state of mind?

I'm currently designing new items in Morocco for our new home here. We're moving from up the mountain hill to an apartment directly on the beach. Such a dream!

If you were to die and come back as a person or a thing, who or what would she/he/it be and why?

I always say I would love to come back as a manta ray, as I find their movements so majestic. The feeling of being in the ocean and exploring its beauty permanently would be incredible.

If you could change one thing about yourself, what would it be?

Right now, that would be my daily routine. I've become so laid-back, I need to regain my power and strength mentally and physically. I can't wait to move closer to the ocean and to start off my day with an early morning surf and swim!

What is your greatest regret?

Not living in Indonesia for a year when I had the chance to. This country stole my heart, and I will definitely return the minute I am able to travel there again.

What is your most treasured possession?

That would definitely be my collection of souvenirs that I've collected from all my trips during the past decade. From silver cutlery that I found at a market in Paris and a handmade palm bag from the islands of

Polynesia, to custom made ceramics from Bali, they all have their own magical story to tell.

What is the quality you most like in a man?

Integrity.

What is the quality you most like in a woman?

Self-confidence.

What do you consider your greatest achievement?

Finding the man I love. Being a creative person with an open-minded spirit and a generous dose of self-confidence, it has not been easy to find a partner that accepts all of my traits. After some hard experiences, I had almost lost my faith in love. I feel so blessed I met Jaouad and that he fully appreciates my craziness, creativity and (sometimes) stubborn mind.

What is your motto?

Explore the world with your eyes wide open, be wild, be curious and fully experience all that is given around you.

8

Emma Mills

AUTHOR, MEDITATION EXPERT

Meditation has become the buzzword of recent times. As it has entered our mainstream, it has gradually gained acceptance as an effective and natural method for trying to live a calmer, longer and more fulfilled life.

Yet what is meditation truly? While it may draw up images of monks tucked away in Himalayan monasteries, and of hours spent sitting cross-legged trying to stop your thoughts, author Emma Mills describes it best: it is 'the practice of moving your attention from the outside world to your inner presence.'

While Emma is known for being an award-winning author and a leading voice in meditation and wellness circles internationally, it is her radiant, grounded and joy-filled energy that truly makes a mark when you meet her.

Her first book, 'Inhale, Exhale, Repeat' published by Penguin Random House, is an insightful and practical guide that seeks to show you just how easy it can be to insert a meditative practice - no matter how brief - across your day.

What is your idea of perfect happiness?

This question reminds me of the first few stanzas from the poem 'Like This' by Rumi.

What is your current state of mind?

Mystified.

If you were to die and come back as a person or a thing, who or what would she/he/it be and why?

An oak tree, perhaps?

If you could change one thing about yourself, what would it be?

To not be allergic to pets - I'd love to have a dog.

What is your greatest regret?

I don't have a greatest regret, they're all great in their own way.

What is your most treasured possession?

Life.

What is the quality you most like in a man?

I like so many qualities, and I also like to be surprised and inspired by new lovely qualities when they arise. Kindness, generosity, patience, compassion, wisdom, intelligence, enthusiasm, a sense of adventure, courage, sensitivity, an appreciation for artistic beauty and spiritual life, sense of humour, authenticity, having a 'can do' attitude.

What is the quality you most like in a woman?

All of the same, as above.

What do you consider your greatest achievement?

I don't have a 'greatest achievement' as they are all great in their own way.

What is your motto?

I don't have a motto. Maybe I have a new motto every day? Right now, it's 7am on a Tuesday morning on the first day of December, and the sky is still dark outside. The moon is full and bright. The stars are out. That's all, and it's just so beautiful.

9

Emmelyn Gunawan

FOUNDER OF CANAAN

My first encounter with Emmelyn Gunawan's grounded, connected, and positive retail vision occurred by pure chance during an afternoon spent exploring The Katamama hotel grounds, one of the few genuinely Balinese corners that are now left in Seminyak. In this tiny oasis, quietly tucked away beneath a low-rise, hand-pressed brick facade, lay Canaan - a boutique brimming with carefully selected, high quality Indonesian lifestyle wares and fashion items set against the earthy, wooden hues of its interiors.

Today, Canaan has evolved into a multi-faceted concept that promotes a sustainable, slow, and local vision that supports crafts and wares of the highest levels. Since opening her first store in 2016, Emmelyn has expanded to open a second Canaan boutique and café opened in partnership with Rou Coffee, and experimental space, Niniveh, in Jakarta, created in collaboration with husband and photographer Chris Bunjamin.

Described by *Condé Nast Traveller* as 'one of the top ten shopping gems of Bali', Canaan inspired a journey that has taken Emmelyn beyond the pure retail sphere to pursue an experiential vision. A stone's throw away from the first Canaan boutique lies Escalier, set in the infamous Potato Head Beach Club. Here, Emmelyn champions premium fashion that is innovative and cutting-edge, introducing niche and recognised brands to the local market.

She expands the Canaan philosophy into workshops, pop-up events and talks aimed at showcasing all that is beautiful and unique from the world of Indonesian craftsmanship. Her considered, value-based vision is an example of how beauty may be found and celebrated close to home, if one looks carefully and closely enough.

What is your idea of perfect happiness?

I think nowadays, if I get a good 8 hours of sleep, I'm very happy - coupled with a quiet morning before I start working.

What is your current state of mind?

I think it's always between a state of excitement because of the future projects, and a state of anxiety because I worry if I've given my all and whether everyone around me is happy with the work that I do.

If you were to die and come back as a person or a thing, who or what would she/he/it be and why?

I think I want to come back as my mom and re-live her life - she could've achieved so much more if she wasn't so restricted by her parents' traditional upbringing. There are positive attributes that I learned from my mother but she does it twice better, so imagine what we could've done together!

If you could change one thing about yourself, what would it be?

I would take everything with a pinch of salt and laugh more.

What is your greatest regret?

I wished I trusted myself more and listen to my gut feeling more often. I have been consumed by greed a number of times, and I have paid greatly.

What is your most treasured possession?

My health. I've struggled with depression before so I know that my health and my state of mind are the most important things.

What is the quality you most like in a man?

Loyalty.

What is the quality you most like in a woman?

A loving heart.

What do you consider your greatest achievement?

With all the work that I do, if I were to lose everything tomorrow I think I'd be ok with it, as I would come to realize that those are merely 'things'. I could wake up tomorrow and start all over again and it would be fine, because I've gone through it before. I have had something so dear to me taken, and having gone through the heartbreak, I am now able to say I've lived it and I can move on - wiser.

What is your motto?

Leaders are those who dare to make their dreams come true!

My mama wrote that for me.

10

Filippo Anzalone

FOUNDER OF BJØRK

Florence never fails to surprise. While famous for its Renaissance history and the magnificence of its culture, art, and architecture that have shaped the cityscape for centuries, tucked away in its folds hide gems spearheading a contemporary vision. Gems such as concept store BJØRK, founded by creative director, Filippo Anzalone.

Located on a quiet lane in hip and happening Santo Spirito, a quarter that has become home to the city's creatives and makers, BJØRK exudes a less-is-more atmosphere. Offering an impeccable selection of niche fashion and accessories labels alongside independent publications from across the world, the space is a celebration of all things minimal and essential with a focus on quality and timelessness.

From established brands such as Studio Nicholson to emerging names rooted in craft and innovation such as Alighieri, BJØRK is as well-placed in Florence as it would be in the streets of New York, Sydney, or London, where Filippo once lived.

As the pandemic has pushed us to face a radical shift in the way the fashion world works and the way we connect with the industry, it will be innovative individuals such as Filippo who will be leading the way in this new world where considered fashion choices will be made.

What is your idea of perfect happiness?

Perfect happiness is being at ease with yourself and being able to enjoy your life to the fullest.

What is your current state of mind?

Rather concerned and worried about the uncertainty of life nowadays both on a personal and professional point of view.

If you were to die and come back as a person or a thing, who or what would she/he/it be and why?

I'd like to reincarnate into a clock in order to have the slight hope to be able to control and manage time.

If you could change one thing about yourself, what would it be?

My lack of self-esteem.

What is your greatest regret?

Doubting myself too much in everything that I do.

What is your most treasured possession?

Raf, my little dog!

What is the quality you most like in a man?

Empathy.

What is the quality you most like in a woman?

Empathy.

What do you consider your greatest achievement?

Being perceived as a kind person.

What is your motto?

Choose to be the best version of yourself.

11

Fred Rigby

FURNITURE AND INTERIORS DESIGNER

Several summers ago, I stepped through the doors of Villa Lena, a creative bolthole that is hidden atop a hill deep in the Tuscan country-side. The tones and balance of its interior aesthetics evoked the warmth of returning home, speaking of a connection to and reverence for nature.

It was only when I came across an aptly-named couch – the Cloud Sofa – in a décor magazine several years later that I realised who had created and designed those remarkable Tuscan interiors: Fred Rigby.

The shapes and tones of the natural world have incessantly fascinated Fred. From his childhood spent exploring the sloped fields and verdant terrains of Dorset, he has threaded a symbiotic connection with nature, transposing this into the fluid lines and tactile textures that characterize his furniture.

Fred's London studio is where his design concepts emerge from; creations that seek to draw us back towards the gentle rhythms of the earth, all while inviting moments of considered reflection on our place in the world.

Since opening his first London studio back in 2012, Fred's impeccable craftsmanship, reserved demeanour, and grounded spirit have attracted the attention of affirmed creatives and brands that share his values, including *Cereal* magazine co-founder and owner of Francis Gallery, Rosa Park, as well as House of Grey founder, Louisa Grey.

More recently, Fred has opened his first showroom in the heart of London Fields, offering a space where visitors can touch, feel and discover all of his crafted pieces. With its 'home from home' vibe, the space reflects his love of the countryside and for design elements that are inspired by a life lived close to nature.

As we continue to be confronted with the importance of respecting our natural world, it is designers such as Fred that will continue to illuminate how deep a connection we may forge with nature indoors.

What is your idea of perfect happiness?

In work, happiness for me is seeing a project being completed, while also seeing the happiness of everyone whom I have worked closely with to accomplish this with. On a personal note, happiness is being surrounded by friends and family and making the most of time off with them while enjoying the smaller things in life, such as going for a walk. One can easily forget about these small but incredibly important aspects when living in a place such as London that is switched on 24/7.

What is your current state of mind?

I feel positive that things are going to change for the better, while I am content with the work that we are producing at the moment. I'm trying not to focus too much on everything else that is going on around us that is related to the pandemic.

If you were to die and come back as a person or a thing, who or what would she/he/it be and why?

An animal that relishes and has freedom – freedom to run and explore and do what it naturally wishes to do.

If you could change one thing about yourself, what would it be?

Not to get so caught up in the moment and to focus on the future.

What is your greatest regret?

On a personal note, not having spoken to my grandparents more before they passed away.

What is your most treasured possession?

My brain.

What is the quality you most like in a man?

Friendship.

What is the quality you most like in a woman?

Friendship.

What do you consider your greatest achievement?

Upholding an entrepreneurial spirit and setting up my business. It has been incredibly rewarding watching it grow over the years with each successful project, while constantly seeking to improve our work with each step forward taken.

What is your motto?

Measure twice, cut once.

12

Gabriela Salord and Nuria Val

CO-FOUNDERS OF ROWSE

Gabriela Salord and Nuria Val exude an energy that is at once radiant and wholesome – it is almost impossible to remain indifferent to their subtle magnetism. This very magnetism is what infuses their line of plant-based skincare and wellness products that bear the ROWSE label, which they co-founded back in 2018.

A chance encounter in Paris brought them together to launch ROWSE with a single product – one that would later become one of their best sellers – the Winter Body Oil. As with all of their formulations that would later evolve from this first creation, it harnesses the potent properties of plants within a handful of raw, non-synthetic elements that are carefully blended with the intention of enhancing our skin's natural state.

"We created ROWSE for those who, like us, are not beauty experts, but who still seek to embrace a conscious approach to beauty and wellness that is simple yet genuinely effective."

ROWSE speaks of Nuria and Gabriela's reverence for plants, while reflecting their diverse personal paths that have connected in synergy through the brand. It is the embodiment of a rare combination of a balanced aesthetic, an honest attitude, and impeccable quality, all whilst remaining rigorously true to its purpose – that of connecting people with the planet through their skincare and wellness rituals.

What began as a side project has transformed into a 14-strong team that works from the newly opened ROWSE headquarters in the creative district of Poblenou. The space, designed by Isern Serra, is a short stroll away from Barcelona's beaches, and captures an energy that only nature has the power to convey.

What is your idea of perfect happiness?

Finding balance, emotionally, intellectually, and physically. It's not an easy quest, but there are moments where we feel we've found it and it's just delicious.

What is your current state of mind?

Aware, conscious, engaged.

If you were to die and come back as a person or a thing, who or what would she/he/it be and why?

We'd love to relive our same lives again, if that could be possible.

If you could change one thing about yourselves, what would it be?

To be less anxious and learn how to go with the flow.

What is your greatest regret?

No regrets so far!

What is your most treasured possession?

Our daughters! Not that we possess them :)

What is the quality you most like in a man?

One that is not threatened by strong-minded women.

What is the quality you most like in a woman?

 Woman or man, we love intelligent, fun and empathetic humans.

What do you consider your greatest achievement?

Building ROWSE in a way that it has become a life project. In this space, we only interact with people we admire; work with plants that inspire us, fuel a positive work atmosphere where we are trying to show that it's possible to be both mothers and entrepreneurs, and find a sort of balance in life.

What is your motto?

Never take no for an answer!

13

Ingrid Opstad

FOUNDER OF THAT SCANDINAVIAN FEELING

For Ingrid Opstad, hygge can be found everywhere. After moving from London to Italy in the name of *amore*, she drew upon her love for writing and her Norwegian roots to launch That Scandinavian Feeling.

What began as a side-project soon evolved into an award-winning editorial platform showcasing Ingrid's personal selection of all those quiet and cozy details that create the unmistakable hygge lifestyle. Her editorial approach is unique, for she celebrates her love for Scandinavian minimalism in all of its forms - from interiors and travel to food and music - while based outside of Scandinavia. Like her Nordic-enamoured readers, she too is looking from the outside in, all while keeping her heritage close to her heart.

Embracing her essence fully and wholeheartedly; genuinely and without the desire to follow trends-of-the-moment, Ingrid is doing more than just sharing her love for hygge. In expressing her interpretation of its aesthetic with the world, she shows us that when we remain true to ourselves, everything unfolds with such ease that our fullest potential cannot help but come to light.

What is your idea of perfect happiness?

To me, perfect happiness is achieved by enjoying the simple moments without focusing on always seeking more. It is about being content with your life and what you already have.

What is your current state of mind?

Calm and happy.

If you were to die and come back as a person or a thing, who or what would she/he/it be and why?

I would have to say my dog, Bowie. To me, he has the perfect cozy life with no worries. He knows the importance of slowing down, he doesn't need much to be happy, and he is always there when you need him - I think we can all learn a thing or two from dogs about life.

If you could change one thing about yourself, what would it be?

As a foreigner living in Italy, I wish I could speak better Italian because it would make my life a lot easier, but it just seems to be a block for me to learn it properly. I am so used to speaking and writing English all day long, and I need to push myself more to find time to learn it.

What is your greatest regret?

I don't have any regrets in life, because even if I have made some bad decisions along the way, they got me to where I am now and I wouldn't change a thing about that.

What is your most treasured possession?

I try not to feel too attached to objects in my life, so can I say my fiancé and my dog? If I have to say a thing that I treasure, then it has to be the PH 5 lamp by Poul Henningsen that I have in my kitchen. This exact one used to hang in my parent's kitchen when I grew up, so it brings up lots of lovely memories around the dinner table and makes me feel connected to them even though they are in Norway and I am here in Italy. Every time I sit down for a meal, I see it and think of them.

What is the quality you most like in a man?

Kindness.

What is the quality you most like in a woman?

Kindness. No matter if it is a man or a woman - I am always looking for the same qualities. No matter who it is, if they are kind, it reflects in everything they do; their ability to listen, to care, to be there for you and to be a friend.

What do you consider your greatest achievement?

I would say creating That Scandinavian Feeling and building the brand up from nothing, with help from my fiancé. From being just an idea many years ago to what it has become today, I feel proud to see my website growing and winning 'Best Written Blog' at an award show in London along the way. It's testament to all the hard work I have put into it so far.

What is your motto?

'Enjoy the little things in life' - because we can easily get caught up in wanting and needing more but in the end, those little moments are the ones worth cherishing.

14

James Reka

ARTIST

What emerges from the hands of artist James Reka is instantly recognizable. His work - be it sweeping outdoor murals or smaller canvases and sculptures - holds a distinct energy that is defined by intersecting spaces, curved angles, and a bold use of the entire colour spectrum. This energy is manifested in wisps of feminine nudes; fragments of animals, fruits and plants, and pure geometric shapes that emerge from his chosen creative medium.

Originally from Melbourne, over the last two decades, James has established himself as a leading figure in the contemporary art scene both within and without Australia. Influenced and inspired by the independent street art movement, as well by pop culture, surrealism, nature, and the people, customs and landscapes of his travels, James's work - while wide-ranging in subject and form - always seeks to connect with its surroundings and with the individuals that interact with his pieces. His work may be seemingly abstract and fantastical, but dig a little deeper, and you will always discover a precise, intentional story; a *fil rouge* that runs throughout.

His work is permanently exhibited at the National Gallery of Australia in Canberra, and his solo shows have been held in galleries and creative spaces globally, from the United States to France, Italy, Switzerland, South Korea, and the United Kingdom. James has collaborated with the likes of Ultimate Ears and Tiffany & Co. and lent his aesthetic to collaborative projects such as the Vision Arts Festival, always remaining true to himself and to his essence.

Having met James several years back, I have always admired how he has consistently cultivated, refined and developed a distinct artistic voice that does not fit within a specific box - his style is not strictly definable. In being so fluid and free, James shows us how no matter how our surroundings may shape-shift, the key to creative fulfilment is held by our inner voice and not by what lies outside of us.

What is your idea of perfect happiness?

It's a well-known quote that "Happiness comes from within." I am a firm believer that you have to make your own self happy, and not rely on other people. I guess the definition of "perfect happiness" could be both of those elements fused together. Being surrounded by a network of friends that truly know you and family obviously helps! For me, it's important to love what you do for a living and make it a passion. This is truly how you can make yourself happy, through satisfaction of one's self.

What is your current state of mind?

After 8 years of living and working out of Berlin, I recently moved to Malta. Packing up my life in Berlin, not just physically but also emotionally, was quite stressful and did cause a lot of anxiety. The last month has been an emotional rollercoaster and a very strange mixture of being excited and scared; of being happy and sad - all at the same time. The positive outcome of this is that these strong emotions have made me feel the most alive I have felt in a long time - most probably since relocating to Berlin from my hometown of Melbourne in Australia almost a decade ago. After successfully relocating and seeing that all the effort was worth it, I am the happiest I have been in years. I am looking forward to seeing how this positive state of mind will reflect not just on my work, but also on my life in general. Also, I am very much looking forward to seeing how Malta inspires me and how my artwork will evolve. Travel is truly the best inspiration, in my opinion.

If you were to die and come back as a person or a thing, who or what would she/he/it be and why?

Since I was young, I have always had these recurring vivid dreams of flying. While this can be a common dream for many, it has always really resonated with me. I know this can be interpreted in many different ways, but for me, I believe I was a bird in a previous life. If we are discussing reincarnation and if I was a bird, I currently must have good karma to now be reincarnated as a human in this life! It might sound strange, but perhaps I would like to become an animal again, possibly a whale or a dolphin. I would assume that being in the ocean would be somewhat peaceful and liberating.

If you could change one thing about yourself, what would it be?

I tend to overthink things, which causes me anxiety and I can be quite pessimistic at times. It's funny, I often expect the worst and I am constantly surprised that it is never as bad as what I have imagined it would be! I have partaken in meditation before, however it's getting to the stage I need to practise this daily and make it a routine to see results. I know I have the ability to change.

What is your greatest regret?

I don't live in regrets - it's destructive and will only bring sadness.

What is your most treasured possession?

I'm not very materialistic. I guess moving around the world has made me ruthless with my possessions, and I tend to always cull down what I own. I do have a couple of treasured ornaments that my Mum gave me when I originally left Melbourne 8 years back. I have two brass Thai elephants and a white marble Chinese Buddha, which have travelled with me around the world. I view them as guardians, and it is always grounding for me to see them. In some way, I view them as home.

What is the quality you most like in a man?

Secure and confident, but not arrogant.

What is the quality you most like in a woman?

Empathy and compassion.

What do you consider your greatest achievement?

Undoubtedly being able to survive as an artist and live from a passion that I would actually do, regardless of making money or not. I feel that should be the goal in life - to fully live one's purpose. My greatest achievement is having relocated to the other side of the world and integrated, whilst still being able to survive off this passion.

What is your motto?

Simplify your life.

15

Karmen Tang

FOUNDER OF ANOTHER STARTUP STORY

Talented and multi-faceted, Karmen Tang embodies perseverance, a global-minded spirit, and a vision projected towards greatness.

A former qualified accountant who was raised in Southampton, worked in London, and holds Hong Kong heritage, Karmen gave up her role at a global advertising agency to launch another startup story - a media platform and consultancy that guides creatives in their entrepreneurial journey. With storytelling at its heart, another startup story strives to serve inspiration and education that is both practical and honest.

From co-hosting informative panel talks with the likes of Javier Perez of Grain Traders fame and media personality Nadia Anya, to releasing podcasts featuring guests such as Peter Bone and Eshita Kabra, Karmen's work has attracted a global audience of the positively informed and inspired.

A deep calling towards understanding what motivates individuals at the emotional level defines her work. In this way, Karmen supports early-stage entrepreneurs to unpack the challenges and opportunities that emerge throughout the business-building process. Above all, Karmen looks to highlighting the importance of empathy and of its fundamental role in the success of any business venture. Ultimately, without heart, a business just moves money, not emotions.

What is your idea of perfect happiness?

From a macro-level, as Simon Sinek says, I imagine a world in which the vast majority of us wake up inspired, feel safe at work and return home fulfilled at the end of the day. Imagine how much better the world would be if this were the case.

From a micro-level, it would be when my mind reaches a complete and utter state of peace. No limiting beliefs, self-destructive thoughts or deep-rooted traumas holding me back from becoming the best version of myself.

What is your current state of mind?

Intention. Being intentional about where I'm spending my time, who with and doing what and consistently asking myself 'what is the purpose of this?'

If you were to die and come back as a person or a thing, who or what would she/he/it be and why?

Nelson Mandela. Of course I don't wish to go through what he did, but I want to emphasise how poorly the man was treated and having gone through all the degradation and humiliation, he allowed it all to develop him, to strengthen him and to open him. He's become one of our great symbols of forgiveness and peace.

'People must learn to hate, and if they can learn to hate, they can be taught to love, for love comes more naturally to the human heart than its opposite.' – Nelson Mandela

If you could change one thing about yourself, what would it be?

To live in the present more and to stop stressing about the future.

What is your greatest regret?

I never regret, I believe all experiences can be used as lessons to shape who you are today in any shape or form.

What is your most treasured possession?

The Bible. The word has changed my whole perspective on life, and consequently how I live life.

What is the quality you most like in a man?

Integrity.

What is the quality you most like in a woman?

Unapologetic

What do you consider your greatest achievement?

Creating another startup story as a source where early-stage entrepreneurs can be educated and inspired to follow their dreams and passions, to be bold and to be encouraged to start today.

What is your motto?

Your mind is the most powerful tool and if trained well, can achieve great things.

Kaye Dong

FOUNDER OF THE NEW MOON

It was the clean-lined aesthetic and calming energy of its website's visuals that drew my eye to The New Moon. I didn't know it then, but its Hong Kong-based founder Kaye Dong had just put the finishing touches on its online shop, seeking to bring a space of respite and tranquillity in the midst of a raging global pandemic.

While it offers a curated selection of items and insightful articles that seek to reconnect us to ourselves and to a grounded sense of spirituality, it is the open-heartedness of Kaye herself that shines through The New Moon and truly distinguishes it from all others.

Holistic health and wellness has become an increasingly important part of our lives, as more of us are appreciating the significance of nurturing every aspect of our being. Without a health-filled body and sense of self, materiality holds little purpose. Conscious of this, Kaye launched The New Moon, stocking an array of objects - such as crystals, sculptural incense holders, oracle cards and books - that are delivered to all continents, while offering experiences to the Hong Kong-based community that educate on wellness-related topics such as kinesiology and gut health. For its global audience, The New Moon provides insights on the lunar cycle and how the universe's constellations impact our every day through regular Instagram-live sessions and posts, reminding us of how we are all interconnected to nature and the cosmos.

Most significantly, The New Moon is fuelled by the same energy that fuels Kaye's other projects, namely her interior design firm The Good Studio, and her child-focussed non-profit foundation, K for Kids - each one reflecting a differing facet of Kaye's essence, while all underpinned by the same values supportive of a genuine, holistic, coherent and positively impactful life.

What is your idea of perfect happiness?

My idea of happiness is when I know I have made someone happy. My happy hormones go wild when I do something for someone I love and see their faces light up with joy. This just gives me so much motivation and purpose in life. Sometimes, these acts are more planned and intentional, but more often than not, they are spontaneous.

What is your current state of mind?

I am multi-passionate by nature, which means I'm always coming up with new ideas and in constant state of change. This does not always make sense to others, but I have been learning to trust my intuition more and prioritise my own joy. Meditation has really helped me stay connected to this source of inner wisdom. So, even though there are lots of changes going on in my life right, I feel calm and content.

If you were to die and come back as a person or a thing, who or what would she/he/it be and why?

I would like to come back as a spiritual guru and help people reconnect with the truth of whom they are.

If you could change one thing about yourself, what would it be?

I think it would be the unrealistically high expectations I set upon myself. This can get me into trouble sometimes, as I unknowingly project these expectations onto others. I am getting better at this, though, by giving myself permission to make mistakes and knowing that this is part of the learning process. I also remind myself that whilst achievement can be a good thing, that alone is not what defines me as a human being.

What is your greatest regret?

I cannot think of any regrets.

What is your most treasured possession?

Definitely all my memories with family and friends!

What is the quality you most like in a man?

Generosity. I admire a man who is generous with his time, his presence, his skills, his wisdom, and his willingness to help and give.

What is the quality you most like in a woman?

Gracefulness. I admire a woman who can carry herself with dignity and can stand tall with compassion and humility. There is a clear focus and purpose in her life, so her poise comes from true, authentic inner confidence.

What do you consider your greatest achievement?

Raising my children, which includes my 2 daughters and all 7 of my foster children.

I went into motherhood absolutely clueless and certainly had no idea what I was getting myself into when I signed up to be a foster caregiver. But, I look at my girls now and feel proud of the confident, generous, fun-loving and compassionate young women that they have become. And I look at all my foster children and feel grateful of the opportunity to have loved and cared for them when they needed it the most.

We did good.

What is your motto?

Make it simple, but significant.

17

Marta Abbott and Nicolas Denino

ARTISTS

What immediately struck me was the setting. The architectural swirls and beauty of its peeling walls and their washed-out tones, the Baroque church of Madonna del Carmine on the outskirts of Lucca set a magnificent contrast to the easels that caught my eye. This, I discovered, was the latest installation and the first joint collaborative project by creatives Nicolas Denino and Marta Abbott entitled 'Liminal Forms'. Co-curated by Caterina Licitra and Lorenzo Belli, the exhibition sought to capture the ephemerality of transitory states.

The personal journeys of both Nicolas and Marta are multi-faceted and fascinating ones: born in Montevideo and with extensive experiences in the worlds of fashion and design that have taken him across Uruguay, Europe and then New York, Nicolas is now based in Italy between Milan and Florence. His work is an exploration of the sense of anxiety that shapes contemporary society, creating circular forms in blue shades across differing media that represent the difficulties of connectedness that this anxiety creates.

Equally as diverse and eclectic, Marta was born in Holland and raised between the United States and the Czech Republic. Her path drew her to live in New York before settling in Rome, where she is now based. Her creative work reflects her fascination with the natural world, using paper and canvas as a backdrop to her interpretation of the nuances that are hidden within our ever-transforming relationship with nature.

While creatively very diverse, Marta and Nicolas have woven their common threads together and explored the transitory space of the liminal to create four distinct artworks that have been created with shades of blue ink. The result is a creative energy that reflects translucence and the beauty of all that transforms.

What is your idea of perfect happiness?

Marta Abbott (MA): I don't know if I carry an idea an idea of perfect happiness necessarily, but I am usually happiest when I'm in the full swing of creating or when I'm by the sea.

Nicolas Denino (ND): When I am experimenting and I see optimal results. When I meet my loved ones.

What is your current state of mind?

MA: Peripatetic.

ND: Liminal state.

If you were to die and come back as a person or a thing, who or what would she/he/it be and why?

MA: I think I might like to come back as a cloud so that I could travel all around the globe with grand views of both land and sky, and so that once in a while I could turn to rain, travel back down to Earth and touch the ocean.

ND: To be the sea, because I think it represents me. Free, deep, calm and furious.

If you could change one thing about yourself, what would it be?

MA: Perhaps the desire to change things about myself! I am currently doing my best to learn more patience, though.

ND: I would like to have more patience.

What is your greatest regret?

MA: I don't like to focus too much on regrets, but I do live according to the belief that you regret the things you do not do more than the things that you do.

ND: Not having spent more time with my grandmother.

What is your most treasured possession?

MA: A painting my son made for me.

ND: Being curious.

What is the quality you most like in a man?

MA: Honesty and a sense of humour.

ND: Honesty and helpfulness.

What is the quality you most like in a woman?

MA: Honesty and a sense of humour.

ND: Honesty and helpfulness.

What do you consider your greatest achievement?

MA: My son, Oliver.

ND: My happiness.

What is your motto?

MA: When in doubt, say yes.

ND: Sharing is caring in my language. *Compartir es vivir.*

18

René Romen

CHOCOLATIER

If a brand name were to be used to define the meaning of provenance, 58chocolate would be it. Born and raised in Merano (in house number

58, of course), founder René Romen crafts his chocolate bars solely with beans that have been rigorously sourced from fair trade growers.

Tucked away in a cobblestoned alleyway in Merano that once housed the city's first artisanal laboratories, this minimalist chocolate atelier serves up a considered range of crafted bars and seasonal additions that include pralines, hot cocoa and cookies. For René, his creations are an opportunity to connect with us, evoking positive emotions with every bite. "When eating my chocolate, I want people to feel happiness. It's a privilege to even be here, in this moment, so let's enjoy this bar of chocolate that has been made with love and joy together."

With its eye-catching and distinct branding, René's chocolate brand is one that captures his personality and story while remaining true to the values of impeccable craftsmanship and quality - all without forgetting a dash of humour.

What is your idea of perfect happiness?

Having the freedom to be creative and being able to realise my ideas. Also knowing that my family is well and that everyone is healthy.

What is your current state of mind?

Full of ideas, sometimes too many, and then I get lost in my thoughts.

If you were to die and come back as a person or a thing, who or what would she/he/it be and why?

I would like to resurrect as a piece of art that leaves many questions open - a piece that no one can understand what its artist was thinking at the time, and yet which they can't stop staring at.

If you could change one thing about yourself, what would it be?

I am grateful and happy for the way I am. As everyone else, I do have my flaws but they make me uniquely who I am.

What is your greatest regret?

I don't have any regrets. I guess the mistakes I have made in the past and the ones I will make in the future are part of my life.

What is your most treasured possession?

My private environment: friends, family and my wife.

What is the quality you most like in a man?

There is no peculiarity that separates men from women. I like when people are honest, friendly, and have a good sense of humour.

What is the quality you most like in a woman?

Ditto.

What do you consider your greatest achievement?

Having created my own brand - my little chocolate world.

What is your motto?

Be nice to people, so that they are nice back.

19

Sandra Githinji

DESIGNER

I stopped in my online scrolling tracks when my eyes crossed the regal gaze of a sculptured goddess and her crown bursting with floral blooms. Created by designer Sandra Githinji, I delved deeper to discover that the gaze belongs to Queen Nandi - one of the most significant queens in South African history - and forms part of a collection of vessels conceptualised by Sandra entitled 'Bloom'.

Born in Kenya and raised in Melbourne - where her studio is now based - Sandra herself is the balanced amalgamation of cultures and experiences. 'Bloom' sprung from her desire to manifest into physical form her African heritage and deep reverence for the diverse facets of precolonial Africa, while combining this vision with her distinct aesthetic shaped by her experiences in Australia.

For Sandra, objects are a fascination, for they each hold a story unique unto themselves that speaks of the hands and minds that created them while embodying a distinct purpose. 'Bloom' is set to bring to life the lives of incredible women that were determinant in influencing the social dynamics within historical Africa, retrieving and celebrating these through handcrafted vessels.

The complete collection will see the realisation of a variety of differing vases, which, in the words of Sandra, "physically symbolise the stories of these women who bloomed where they were planted, some through difficult situations, yet they rose and paved the way for many of us today, standing as symbols of the power in women."

What is your idea of perfect happiness?

Self-love and acceptance.

What is your current state of mind?

Grateful. I took a step out into the unknown last year when I launched my independent design practice amidst a global pandemic. The journey has been wondrous. The support I've received from family and friends has been profound, not to mention the community that has been created through the Kickstarter campaign for the project 'Bloom'. I wake up everyday, grateful to be able to create freely, and that the work resonates with people.

If you were to die and come back as a person or a thing, who or what would she/he/it be and why?

It would have to be Doctor Strange so I could travel through time from the beginning of the universe. I've been fascinated with pre-colonial

Africa, and to be able to experience it and live through lost history would be extraordinary.

If you could change one thing about yourself, what would it be?

To retain information. My memory is terrible.

What is your greatest regret?

I don't have regrets - not because I don't wish certain things could have played out differently, but because I fully believe in the course that has been set out before me. That everything I have endured has moulded me to the person I am today. It all matters and because of this, I don't have regrets.

What is your most treasured possession?

My sense of self, free of external commentary.

What is the quality you most like in a man?

Empathy.

What is the quality you most like in a woman?

Empathy.

What do you consider your greatest achievement?

The work I will leave behind.

What is your motto?

Whatever it is you are searching for, it is already in you. Always look inward.

20

Sari Kassouf

FOUNDER OF THE SLOW

While the larger and more obvious metropolises across the world constantly jostle for attention upon the international creative stage, it is those lesser-known corners globally, filled with individuals who are quietly championing a considered way of expressing and showcasing talent, that truly inspire me. Far from the bright lights and distracting cacophony, brands and spaces are emerging that are no-less rooted in excellence and talent than those that are based in what have traditionally been considered creative hubs of greatness.

Lebanon represents one of the finest examples of this movement - often associated by the outside world with difficult scenes of conflict and tension, this breathtakingly diverse sliver of land that overlooks the Mediterranean is in fact a melting pot of exceptional design, creativity and beauty bursting at the seams. Tucked away in Beirut's hip Mar Mikhayel quarter, concept-boutique-cum-cafè The Slow is spearheading a retail and culinary philosophy that has been attracting the attention of those-in-the-know across the world since it opened its doors in November 2019.

It is a reflection of founder Sari Kassouf's unique story - one that is as interesting as it is exceedingly rare. Previously a full-time architect who was practising across the Middle East, a voyage to Bali proved to be a turning point. While on the island, Sari was drawn to the relationship that local creatives nurture with both nature and spirituality. On the island, the natural flow of life is revered, forming an intrinsic part of creative expression. Utterly different to what Sari had been pursuing up until that point, this attitude left a deep impression.

Upon returning to Lebanon, he decided to bring all threads together - his professional experience, his appreciation for simple geometries and pure aesthetics, and his desire to live in harmony with nature - and launch The Slow. Featuring a carefully-selected range of fashion, beauty and design brands that uphold his values, the space is also home to a café that offers the freshest fare rooted in the seasons and the local land. An invitation to slow down and embrace the now, one can't help but fall in love with all that The Slow represents.

What is your idea of perfect happiness?

Slow living is really my idea of perfect happiness. Waking up without an alarm; brewing the most perfect cup of coffee; finding my way to a nice café; sitting under the sun and indulging in a divine breakfast; watching people being a blessing; living in the moment every moment…

What is your current state of mind?

The hidden gem behind the terrace of The Slow, which I'm fantasizing about taking over, renovating, and adding to the space.

If you were to die and come back as a person or a thing, who or what would she/he/it be and why?

I'd probably choose to come back as a Tibetan monk. There's something about living life in solitude and in complete harmony with your natural environment that really appeals to me.

If you could change one thing about yourself, what would it be?

Well, I hate to say it, but I'm a perfectionist. So, I'd change that. It'll probably make my life so much easier.

What is your greatest regret?

I'm so selective when it comes to relationships, which sometimes makes it difficult for me to really open up to people. It's those missed opportunities of connection that I sometimes regret.

What is your most treasured possession?

I am not a materialistic person, but I couldn't help but think of my loved ones when I first read your question. Perhaps it's my memories of them that are my most treasured possession.

What is the quality you most like in a man?

Gentleness.

What is the quality you most like in a woman?

Strength.

What do you consider your greatest achievement?

The fact that I opened The Slow at the cusp of the revolution in Lebanon — which was followed by an economic meltdown that was later made even more severe by the COVID lockdown — and managed to stay in business to this day is truly an achievement.

What is your motto?

You reap what you sow.

Acknowledgements

A heartfelt thank you to Farah Liz Pallaro, who dropped the first pebble that created the first ripple.

Photographic Credits

1. Aude Giraud – © Aude Giraud
2. Anestis Michalis - © Anestis Michalis
3. Beckielou Brown and Bridget Plant - © Roo Kendall
4. Bianca Gregg - © Lynden Foss
5. Clementina Calleri - © Clementina Calleri
6. Cynthia Louise - © Cynthia Louise
7. Daisy Sophia – © Daisy Sophia
8. Emma Mills - © Emma Mills
9. Emmelyn Gunawan - © Nadine Maulida
10. Filippo Anzalone - © Filippo Anzalone
11. Fred Rigby - © Renee Kemps
12. Gabriela Salord and Nuria Val - © ROWSE
13. Ingrid Opstad - © Ingrid Opstad
14. James Reka - © James Reka
15. Karmen Tang - © Karmen Tang
16. Kaye Dong - © Ruby Law
17. Marta Abbott and Nicolas Denino - © Katerina Tan
18. René Romen - © Markus Federspiel
19. Sandra Githinji - © Sergei Pozdniakov
20. Sari Kassouf - © Sari Kassouf

Born in Italy and raised in Singapore, Rossella E. Frigerio is a writer and copywriter who shapes words that reflect her singular life experience.

Previously a legal advisor to Dame Vivienne Westwood and the co-founder of Sofia Capri (a sandal brand that had been much loved by *Vogue Italia's* legendary editor, Franca Sozzani), she is currently writing her first book of fiction. She is represented by Tizian & Canali.